Memories

Rosemary Syvret

Memories © 2022 Rosemary Syvret

All rights reserved.

No part of this publication may be reproduced, stored in a retrieval system, or transmitted, in any form or by any means, electronic, mechanical, photocopying, recording or otherwise, without the prior written permission of the presenters.

Rosemary Syvret asserts the moral right to be identified as author of this work.

Presentation by *BookLeaf Publishing*

Web: www.bookleafpub.com

E-mail: info@bookleafpub.com

ISBN: 9789395255240

First edition 2022

DEDICATION

To my Lovely Husband and My Children from his
One True Love Margaret,Loving Wife and Mother

PREFACE

This is a book written by a well loved Only Daughter
of a Lovely Talented Mother and Wife

The Day An Angel Came

Five years ago this morning
We kissed and I held your hand
But an Angel was hovering
To take you from this Land.
I didn't want to lose you
You didn't want to go
The Heartache that you left behind
No one will ever know.
I loved you when I first saw you
And I love you still
Just being with you My Darling
Gave me such a thrill.
We didn't need material things
To make our world right
A Kiss,a Touch,a Cuddle
We could make it through the night
Our love was very precious
It didn't cost a thing
But we had the Happiness and that meant everything.
Love Always Margaret

55th Wedding Anniversary

I'll always remember the vows we made on that
special Day,
I promised that I would Love,Honour and Obey,
As I look back on these years,just one thing comes to
mind,
If I had searched the whole wide world,a better Man I
wouldn't find.
You were the starlight in my eyes,the reason for my
life,
You gave me five beautiful children,when I became
your Wife,
You made me laugh,you made me cry,you gave me
comfort too,
I know I wasn't perfect, but I tried very hard for you,
If I could have just one Wish,I know what it would
be,
That all the Lovers in this world,could be as happy as
You and Me.
I Miss You so much Darling,life will never be the
same,
But the Love and all the Memories will forever
remain.
So on this very special Day my thoughts are all of
You,
I know that you will give me the Love and Strength
to Carry through
One Day my Darling I will kiss and Hold you tight
Until then My Darling Mike You will be my Guiding
Light.
   God Bless you Darling

To a Special Man on Fathers Day

My Heart still belongs to You,I think of you each
Day,
And Darling,when I'm feeling blue,I often hear You
say,
"When the wind blows look for me,as I gently caress
your Face,
I'm still beside you Darling,My arms around your
waist.
The morning Dew on the roses, Are the tears that I
have shed,
I'm there to Kiss you goodnight when you go to bed,
So don't be sad My Darling,because I never went far,
I am the sunshine in your eyes,I am the evening star.
My presence is all around you,wherever you may go.
I will never leave you,because I love you so.
So have a Happy Fathers Day ,in Heaven up above,
I'm sending lots of Kisses wrapped up with All My
Love.
  Margaret

Happy 77th Birthday Mike

It's that special time of year,once again your
Birthdays here,
Birthdays come and Birthdays go,but I will always
love You so.
We don't have parties anymore,
Now Birthdays are such a Bore.
It's now been 4 Birthdays my love,
That you have spent in Heaven above.
I think about You everyday,the pain and Heartache
won't go away,
There's alot of catching up to do.
But we'll save that until I'm with you.
Every Special birthday was such a delight,
We'd have karaoke and party every night,
I have so much to be thankful for,
And grateful I'll always be,
For the Loving Compassionate Husband,
Who chose to spend his life with Me.
We met when I was just Sixteen,
I knew right from the start,
That you My Darling Michael,
Would never break My Heart.
So please Forgive me Darling,
Now that your Birthdays here,
If on your Special Day,
I shed a Silent Tear.
All My love Margaret

For the most Wonderful Husband

It's been 4years Mike,what can I say,
I've Missed You so much everyday,
I was just 17 when I became your bride
From then you were always by my side.
Everything we did,we did together,
You saw Me through the Stormy Weather,
We made a home filled with Love,
Raised the children sent from Heaven Above.
But our time together never came,
Because an Angel called your name,
I know you were tired of the fight,
It took its toll both day and night,
But we fought it together for 16yrs,
Through the good times and the tears,
You always Smiled,you were never Sad,
You took the good times with the bad.
I know you're still here with Me,
What I would give,if I could see
Your Smiling Face and loving eyes
Your tender touch when you said goodbye
To hold you just One Time More,
To see you walk in through the door.
I Love you Darling,with All My Heart
And even though we are apart
My love for you will never die,
I'll say Hello and not Goodbye.
One Day we'll be together again,
Then sunny skies will block out the rain.
Love Margaret

To My Lovely Husband and Father

It seems like only Yesterday that
you stood by my side,
In Death Love is Eternal,in life you were my Guide,
There are so many things,that I would love to say,
I know that you still hear me in a very special way,
To hold and Kiss you once again,would be such a
delight,
To have you lying next to me throughout the darkest
nights.
Words can't express the way I feel now you have
gone,
I only know my Love for You will live on and on,
And so on Fathers Day,my Darling Mike,
With you in Heaven above,I'm sending a Million
Kisses wrapped up with All My Love.
    Love always Margaret

For my Mike on his Birthday

Today is your 79th birthday,I know that you're not
here,
It's Still a very special Day,and I'll shed a silent tear
The tears are not for sorrow,the tears are not for joy,
The tears Are for what we lost, the day that we lost
you,
We have lots of memories we keep within our Hearts,
We Love You My Darling,even though we're far
apart,
I feel you close beside Me,in everything I do,
I don't think I've told you but Smudgie misses you
too,
Every evening at Bedtime,he waits by the Lounge
door,
He knows it's time to say goodnight to his Daddy
once more.
He loves to sit in the Lounge in your Favourite Chair,
And Look lovingly at your photo on The table there,
Have a lovely birthday in your Home up above
And we'll never Forget you,we're sending you our
love.

Margaret

Merry Christmas Mike

Five years have gone,in the blink of an eye,
But my Love and Memories will never die,
I know you can hear when I speak your name,
But without you My Darling,nothing is the same.
I Miss your loving Smile and your Tender Touch,
Oh My Darling Mike,I Miss you so much,
But life continues although you're not here,
A Few tears will flow among the Christmas cheer,
So My Darling,I'm sending All My Love,
Have a Wonderful Christmas in Heaven above.
  All My Love Margaret

Six year Anniversary of Mike's passing

I can't believe it's been so long,
Since the day we said Goodbye.
The years have simply vanished
In the blinking of an eye.
And yet my hearts still broken,
I thought time was meant to heal,
But knowing that your gone,
Still feels so sad and quite unreal.
For no one else in this world,
Could fill the void you left behind,
You Were a Special Husband,
The very best I could ever find.
And I will Miss You Always,
And I promise you my Love,
That you will live on in My Heart,
As long as the stars shine above.

       Sent with All My Love Margaret

Miracle of Birth

The joy you both have given,
The Happiness you share,
The Wonder of a pair of Arms,
A Baby nestling there.
You prayed for God to send you,
This Dream of Dreams come true,
No Two are more deserving,
To be Parents but you.
God granted you this Miracle,
It Came from Heaven above,
He Gave him/her to you just because,
He knew He/she would be Loved.
No words could ever tell you,
The Happiness we feel,
God Bless you both and keep you,
Your Miracle has become real.

My dog Dandy

I have a dog his name is Dandy,
His eyes are Brown and his coat is Sandy,
His tail is long and his legs are Bandy,
The Best in the world is my dog Dandy.
I took him to the village fair,
There were lots of things to do down there,
I went on Roundabouts and Swings,
And ever so many exciting things,
I ate Sugar Cakes and Candy,
And quite forgot about my Dog Dandy,
Suddenly when I looked around,
Dandy was nowhere to be found,
I asked the Lady selling Candy,
Whether she'd seen My Dog Dandy,
"No" she said "But if I do,I will send him back to
you",
The Policeman at the village fair
Hadn't seen Dandy anywhere there,
People came from miles around,
To show Me the Lost dogs they'd found,
Collies,Terriers and Alsatians,
Spaniels,Labradors and Dalmatians,
Everyone was very kind
To help me my lost dog to find.
A little girl came running up,
And said to me "is this your pup".
I answered "No he's far too small,
He's not like My Old Dog at all"
Sadly I walked home alone,
Wondering where My dog had gone,

Was he laying on a bed of Silk,
Petted by Ladies and fed on milk,
Or had he gone on a trip,
As a Seadog on a ship,
Home I walked and climbed the stairs,
And who do u think was waiting there,
With eyes of brown,
And coat so sandy,
Wagging his tail,
Was my Dog Dandy.
    Margaret Syvret

I know A Little spider

I know a little Spider,he creeps upon the wall,
He makes a pretty little Web,and wastes no time at
all,
He has a small brown body,and thick brown furry
legs,
A little Head and Beady eyes,how fine He spins his
Web.
He watches the flies there playing,and smiles with all
his might,
If they are playing near his Web,My Word!they'll get
a fright,
For Cunning Mr Spider,
Will Run out in Delight.
But Oh!Dear Me,the flies are cute,they just fly out of
sight,
One Day that little Spider was curled up in a heap,I
think he must of broke his heart,
He had no flies to eat.

Margaret Syvret

My childhood days

If I had my childhood days over again,
I'd go to the woods and the meadows to play,
I'd pick buttercups and make daisy chains,
And laugh if I got caught out in the rain,
I'd have birthday treats and plenty to eat,
And invite all the children who live in the street,
And one thing I'd like,and I'm sure mummied agree,
Is to invite the little Lord Jesus to tea.
How nice it would be for us all to be good,
And follow his footsteps as good children should.
  Margaret Syvret

The passing years

Oh! Where oh! Where have my babies gone,oh!
Where oh! Where can they be.
Five minutes ago they were safe in my arms,
Now I can sit on their knee.
From time to time I look back on these days,
With loving tears in my eyes,
It's so unbelievable when children are born,
How fast those years go by.
Babies are very precious we nurture them with care,
They make you laugh they make you cry,
At times we could pull out our hair.
These emotions we go through,
When they are growing away,
Before you know it they have gone,
And it's another day.
The cycle starts over once more,
An ever turning circle of life,
Grandchildren are at the door,
Once more your world is rife.
But we love and we nurture them,
They are such a joy,
We really spoil them rotten,
And buy them lots of toys.
It's just like having your babies home
Your life is no longer a Bore,
The only difference was when you've had enough,
You can send them home once more.

Margaret Syvret

Remembering my Mike.

It doesn't get any easier,it's a lie what they say,
That the pain and the heartache will one day fade
away.
For you My Darling Michael will never be forgot,
You were my life my everything,in life you were my
Rock.
I know you're still beside me in everything I do,
But life will never be the same,you see I still Love
You.
Those sad films that we used to watch would fill your
eyes with tears,
You'd get up and walk away saying "I'll put the kettle
on Dear,"
Do u remember the pampas grass on the front lawn,
Now it is no longer it looks so forlorn.
The pampas grass needs seeing too of that there is no
doubt,
The centre of it is so dry we need to sort it out,
I've read we need to burn it so that is what i'Il do,
Only the dry bits will burn,it'll be as good as new.
Well burn it did for most of the day,I'll never forget
the scene,
But it looked like a burnt hedgehog,
Where the pampas grass had been.
Then there was the day when shopping needed doing,
While I was out you decided that my piano was
going,
A Breakfast bar is what we need
For our children now they are growing.

That pianos in the way I'll move it without her
knowing.
When I came home from shopping,
The dining room looked bare,
Oh where is my piano, it should be standing there,
Then I heard you working very hard in the back
garden,
But the shock I had when I got there made me so
disheartened.
There was My piano laying in the grass,
All in bits and pieces,"what have you done," I asked,
I'm going to build a breakfast bar,it's really what we
need,
That piano was taking the space
Where the children could sit and feed,
I'll keep the wood and the hinges,they're too good to
throw away,
They'll come in very handy to use another day.
I really couldn't get angry,I always did forgive
For there was always a purpose in everything you
did.
One Day I bought some Daffodils to brighten up the
home,
They would look lovely in the crystal vases My mum
used to own,
I should of known better but then I didn't see
The cupboard was empty where the vases should be,
They were taking up needed space,and wasn't used as
such,
You gave them to the dustman,they said "thank-you
very much,
No vases for the daffodils,oh what shall I do,

You said "don't worry I have the answer for you",
There's a cupboard full of empty jars,you use when making jam,
Just stick the daffodils in them,make use of them while u can.
So now I had jam jars where crystal vases should be,
But I Still loved you dearly that's how it was with me.
Everything over the years have been replaced with Care,
Except for you My Darling ,if only I could replace you there.
Everything can be bought in shops,
But a person dies,once the heart stops.
You cannot replace a love so true,
It doesn't matter what you do.
So cherish your loved ones while you live,
Think of all the pleasure it gives,
Because one day you Will be,
With just your memories like me.
  Love always Margaret

Growing old

Why is old age so lonely?why is it such a bore?
Why because you're getting old,no-one wants you
anymore?
As a Mother and a Wife you give your very best,
Perhaps it's just because they think u need a rest.
Once children ran riot in your home,
Now you'll be really lucky,if they pick up the phone.
Yes we know they have their own lives and they work
everyday,
But we gave up our lives just to help them on their way.
When we should be enjoying life,we're left all alone,
With just our memories,if only we had known.
We never thought that we would be so lonely in our
lives,
Some have lost their Husbands and some have lost their
Wives.
So All you children out there,who have parents still
alive,
Be grateful for the love and care that they gave you all
your lives.
Remember that although,you've left them All alone,
They still need love and hugs and it's great to see them
come home,
Don't make them feel unwanted,go see them once in a
while,
Give them something to live for,something to make
them smile.
One Day you Will realise how lonely life can be,
And when that day comes,I know you'll think of me.
Love Mum

Mum

Mum you suffered and hid your pain
Now you're back with Dad again
He'll meet you up at Heaven's Door
And you'll be together forever More.
Tell him we still miss him and Love him so,
Mum it is with Great Sadness that you had to go.
Our feelings of you will always run deep,
Our memories of you both we'll cherish and keep.
God Bless you Mum though we feel the pain,
Although Sad,we're happy knowing that you're back
with Dad once again.
Remembering you both is easy,we do it everyday,
But there's an ache within Our hearts that'll never go
away.
Although the time is never right,
We'll say God Bless to you both with a Kiss
Goodnight.
Love from John,Margaret,Sian,Aaron,Steven
Hayleigh,Kayden & Lily.

Dear Mum

The moment that you Died,
My Heart was torn in two,
One side filled with Heartache,
The other Died with you.
I often lie awake at night,
When all the World's asleep,
And take a walk down Memory Lane,
With Memories that I keep.
Remembering you is easy,
I do it everyday,
But Missing you is Heartache,
That never goes away.
I hold you tightly in my heart,
And there you will remain,
Until my life on earth does end,
When we will meet Again.
Love from Your Daughter Rosie

To Dad

We didn't know that Day,
That God would Call your Name,
In life we loved you dearly,
In Death we do the same.
It broke our hearts to lose you,
But you didn't go alone,
For part of us went with you,
The Day God called you Home.
You left us beautiful Memories,
Your love is still our Guide,
And though we cannot see you,
You're always by our side.
Our Family Chain is broken
And nothing will ever be the same,
But as God calls us one by one,
The chain will link again.
Love from your daughter Rosemary & your Sons
John,Michael,Francis & Robert.

Ode to Michael

My Second Fathers Day without you,
And it still breaks my Heart,
I never thought 2 years ago,
That we would ever part.
I still look for you Each Day,
And wish that you were here,
To take away the Heartbreak,
And wipe away My Tears.
How I Miss You Darling,
No one will ever know
Because My Darling Michael,
I still Love You So.
Your Laugh Was so Infectious,
The Stars Shone in your eyes,
And I will never forget the day,
When I had to say Goodbye,
So if you're looking Down on Me,
From your New Home up Above,
Remember I'll Always Miss You
So I'm sending You All My Love.

Margaret

My Ambition

It's easy when your young they say,
To wish our Childhood Days away,
Well I'm not wishing for the Impossible,
I just want to be like Sebastian Coe,
The Future they say Holds the Three Minute Mile,
One day I'll win that race in style,
Just twelve years old i might be,
But think of the training in front of me
An impossible task!Did I hear you say,
In the next ten years I'll find a way.
That's one record that will be Mine,
And when it is,I think you'll find,
That Syggy will convey the News,
I owe it all to Bideford Blues.
And the ones that trained Me Day And Night,
Three cheers for Geoff Fanson and Chalky White.
They helped with My training all the while,
It's to them I owe the Three Minute Mile.
Their Dedication helped me win through,
Thank God I joined the Bideford Blues.

Margaret syvret

www.ingramcontent.com/pod-product-compliance
Lightning Source LLC
La Vergne TN
LVHW021350200726
843509LV00014B/2773